After you!

By Janine Amos

Illustrated by Annabel Spenceley

CHERRYTREE BOOKS

A Cherrytree Book

Designed and produced
by A S Publishing

First published 1998
by Cherrytree Press Ltd
a subsidiary of
The Chivers Company Ltd
Windsor Bridge Road
Bath BA2 3AX

British Library Cataloguing in Publication Data

Amos, Janine
 After you!. – (Good manners)
 1.Interpersonal relations – Juvenile literature
 I.Title II.Spenceley, Annabel
 395.1'22

ISBN 0 7540 9024 8

Printed and bound in Italy by L.E.G.O. s.p.a., Vicenza

Going to the park

Leroy, Harry and Jamal are going to the park.

They are in a hurry to start their game.

The boys reach the park gate.

So does Mrs King.
The gate is narrow.

Harry and Jamal push through.
The buggy gets stuck.

How does Mrs King feel?

Leroy waits.

How does Mrs King feel now?

Leroy catches up with his friends.

Adam and Tom

Adam and Tom are painting.

They both need to wash their brushes.

The water tips.

The paintings are spoilt.

Adam and Tom start again.

Tom thinks about it.

Next time, Tom waits.

Mr Potter

Sophie and Jess want ice creams.

The shop is busy.

Mr Potter is next.

The big girls take his turn.

How does Mr Potter feel?

Sophie and Jess have their money ready.

The girls think about Mr Potter.

How does Mr Potter feel now?

31

"People like to feel you care about them. Letting someone else go first shows people that you do care. Waiting your turn helps things run smoothly. If someone lets you go first, remember to say Thank you."